MAKE SOMEONE HAPPY

A CREATIVE Journal for BRIGHTENING the WORLD Around you

emily coxhead

A TarcherPerigee Book

tarcherperigee

TarcherPerigee
An imprint of Penguin Random House LLC
375 Hudson Street
New York, New York 10014

Most TarcherPerigee books are available at special quantity discounts for bulk purchase for sales promotions, premiums, fund-raising, and educational needs. Special books or book excerpts also can be created to fit specific needs. For details, write: SpecialMarkets@penguinrandomhouse.com.

ISBN 9780143131540

Printed in the United States of America

1 3 5 7 9 10 8 6 4 2

BOOK DESIGN BY EMILY COXHEAD

THIS BOOK is dedicated To those WHO remind mE THAT the WORLD ISN'T SUCH a BAD PLACE

hii,

I can't promise you that this book holds all the secrets to a happier world. I don't know the answers to make you (or anyone else) happy, I wish I did! I'm not a psychologist or a scientist or somebody who's been through a whole load of life experiences and become an expert on all of these things. I'm just somebody who was a little bit sad one time and decided to do something about it—for myself more than anybody else.

In December 2015 I launched *The Happy Newspaper*, an actual newspaper celebrating only good news. But what began as a silly idea became so much more than that. It probably saved me a tiny bit (not to sound too melodramatic). The newspaper became my focus at a not-so-great time and it's something that brought me heaps of happiness, hope, and love. In turn, it had the exact same effect on so many more people than I could've imagined.

I spoke to strangers who had opened up to me, I wrote open letters to nobody in particular, and it helped! The whole experience opened up my eyes to people—people who had been cracked and glued back together far too many times, and people who were imperfect but absolutely wonderful and magic.

Now I find myself going out of my way to help people whenever I can. When I say "help people", I mean something as simple as a smile or helping somebody with heavy luggage, asking a homeless person if they want some food as I enter a shop. . . . These are TINY, almost insignificant things in the grand scheme of everything. We aren't all able to find a cure for a life-threatening disease or perform surgery on somebody.

But I honestly think that if all of us did more of these tiny, almost insignificant things, the world (or a few people's worlds) would be a much happier place. We can't change huge global problems—we don't get much of a say in the big decisions made in our towns or by our governments—but we definitely have a say in how we treat others on a daily basis.

This book is a reminder that kindness still exists in abundance, that there are strangers helping strangers every single day, in all corners of the planet, and you and I can be a part of that. It can be easy to forget this when we see nothing but terror and fear on our TV screens, on our phones, and, of course, in newspapers, but we can create our own "happy news."

What I'm saying is: You have the ability to change the world, one random act of kindness at a time. . . . how good is that?!

So, whether this book is your therapy, a little companion to remind you you're not alone, or just something to pass the time of day, I hope it brings just a tiny bit of happiness, consideration, and kindness to those around you.

We're going to have the most magic time!

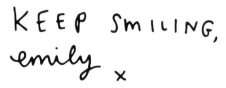

KEEP SMILING,
emily x

FIRSTLY

DON'T FORGET TO
TAKE CARE OF YOU

- ☐ DRINK SOME WATER
- ☐ GET enough SLEEP
- ☐ TAKE A FEW DEEP BREATHS
- ☐ EAT SOMETHING lovely
- ☐ SAY I'm DOING GREAT

I'LL BE CHECKING in ON YOU THROUGHOUT THE BOOK!

THINK OF THE PEOPLE CLOSEST
TO You WHO HAVE BEEN
KIND TO You LATELY

- _____
- _____
- _____
- _____
- _____
- _____
- _____
- _____

TRY TO think OF SOME STRANGERS WHO HAVE BEEN KIND TO you...

(THE PERSON WHO DELIVERED you AS A BABY, etc.)

- _____
- _____
- _____
- _____
- _____
- _____
- _____

NOTICE an ACT OF KINDNESS this WEEK

* describe it below *

"LOOK FOR THE HELPERS... you WILL ALWAYS FIND PEOPLE WHO ARE HELPING."
- MR. ROGERS

Think of SOMEONE you KNOW WHO IS ABSOLUTELY **WONDERFUL** AND **MAGICAL** in ALL KINDS of WAYS...

WRITE DOWN YOUR THREE FAVORITE THINGS ABOUT THEM:

1.

2.

3.

TEXT THEM
...

WRITE THEM A NOTE

call them

AND TELL THEM... THEY MAY NEED TO HEAR IT TODAY!

WRITE a *letter* to YOUR <u>BEST</u>
FRIEND on their <u>VERY WORST DAY</u>...
...LET THEM KNOW EVERYTHING'S GOING TO BE <u>OKAY</u>

SAVE THIS PAGE UNTIL THEY (OR
YOU!) NEED TO HEAR IT.

CUT THESE tiny notes OUT and LEAVE THEM IN PLACES FOR strangers (or PEOPLE you know!) TO FIND...

EVERY -THING WILL BE OKAY!	SOME DAYS ARE A LITTLE BIT FOGGY and THAT'S OKAY... TOMORROW'S A BRAND-NEW DAY	you've GOT THIS... WHAT EVER "THIS" IS!
You DESERVE YOUR LOVE, CARE & ATTENTION JUST as much AS ANYONE else ♡	you're DOING GREAT!! (you REALLY ARE)	you MEAN THE WHOLE WORLD TO SO MANY PEOPLE ♡
		WRITE your OWN

PLACES you could leave THEM:

- LIBRARY BOOK (OR A FRIEND'S book)
- A TAXI
- AT A BUS STOP
- INSIDE a CAFE MENU
- ON A CAR WINDSHIELD
- IN A MAILBOX
- ON A FRIDGE DOOR
- ON A RESTROOM MIRROR

THIS

is what AN <u>EVERYDAY</u>
<u>HERO</u> looks *like*...

← PHOTO
OR DRAWING
(IF YOU'RE
FEELING
BRAVE)

EVERYDAY
HERO

WAHOOOO

<u>EVERYDAY HERO</u>

= SOMEBODY WHO MAKES THE WORLD, OR
YOUR WORLD, a *little* BIT HAPPIER

BREAKING:

WHAT made you ⸻smile⸻
this WEEK IN THE NEWS?

(GO ON, TRY TO FIND SOMETHING)

WE ARE CONSTANTLY
SURROUNDED by THINGS
aiming to DEPRESS US,
whether We're too FAT
or too thin... or SHOULD
HAVE BETTER SKIN.

WE ARE CONSTANTLY
reminded of THE TERROR
AND FEAR HAPPENING ALL
over the WORLD, no matter
HOW FAR or NEAR.

SO, ANYTHING that CAN
SHED a BIT of LIGHT
on WHAT CAN BE A VERY
DARK PLANET... IS SO RARE
and MAGIC like a
BLUE MOON OR a COMET.

WE SHOULD hold ON TO
them like FAIRY DUST
and KEEP THEM the SAFEST...
BECAUSE THEY DON'T HAPPEN
VERY OFTEN and THEY'RE
ABSOLUTELY GOLDEN!

HAVE a CONVERSATION with a SALES
CLERK... ASK THEM HOW THEY ARE
...LEARN ANYTHING INTERESTING?

YAY!

eRm, NO

BEEP

BEEP

HOW MANY FLUFFY ANIMALS did you SEE TODAY?

(INSTAGRAM ACCOUNTS, YOUTUBE VIDEOS, ETC., ALSO COUNT!)

(CLOUD THAT LOOKS LIKE A FLUFFY ANIMAL)

☐ OTHER

☐ GREAT DAY FOR FLUFFY ANIMALS ☺

☐ NOT SO GREAT DAY FOR FLUFFY ANIMALS ☹

YOU ARE ONE IN
OVER 7.4 BILLION
humans on this PLANET
AND ALTHOUGH you
MAY NOT BE ABLE TO
CHANGE THE WHOLE =
WORLD

...you CAN MAKE A FEW
OF THOSE WORLDS a
tiny bit BRIGHTER.

YOU'RE INCREDIBLY APPRECIATED

Dear _____

Thank You So much for
making the WORLD a ~~LITTLE~~ WHOLE
~~bit~~ LOT HAPPIER _____

_____

_____

_____

Love from _____

DIFFICULT CONVERSATIONS DON'T ALWAYS NEED TO BE TERRIFYING

GO ON,
TRY IT YOURSELF...

SPACE TO BREATHE

"ME" TIME

NOTICE A SMALL VICTORY
TODAY & WRITE IT ABOVE

TALK TO AN elderly PERSON TODAY – WHETHER IT'S SOMEBODY you know or a stranger at THE BUS STOP – you MAY BE the ONLY PERSON they SPEAK TO THIS WEEK!

WRITE THEIR PEARLS OF WISDOM HERE:

TALK to SOMEBODY YOUNGER
than you... WRITE THEIR
WORDS of WISDOM HERE:

(OR ask THEM TO WRITE IT)

PICK A STRANGER
(any stranger)

and IMAGINE WHAT their
STORY COULD BE...

(WE ALL have OuR OWN
PRETTY WONDERFUL STORY)

DRAW
THEM

CUT OUT A NEWSPAPER clipping that RESTORED YOUR FAITH in HUMANITY - a tiny bit (STICK IT BELOW)

YAY!
LOVELY
PEOPLE

TEENY tiny little
THINGS I APPRECIATED
TODAY...
(FILL THE PAGE)

PEEP PEEP

etc.

COLOR ME IN

PAY IT FORWARD

WITH FOOD OR DRINK FOR SOMEBODY WHO MAYBE CAN'T AFFORD IT...

CHIPS

JUICE

NEXT TIME YOU'RE GRABBING SOME FOOD OR A DRINK TO GO, WHY NOT PAY FOR THE NEXT PERSON'S DRINK OR SNACK?

HOT CHOC

AN email (OR OTHER INTERNET
"THING") THAT made ME
SMILE LOADS:

FROM:

(REMEMBER TO SEND THEM SOMETHING LOVELY BACK)

hiii how's your
DAY BEEN? I HOPE
IT'S BEEN PACKED full
OF SUNSHINE and RAINBOWS,
SPARKLES and SHINY things,
your FAVORITE FOODS and
OTHER TINY TWINKLY things

you learn SOMETHING
NEW EVERY DAY

(or at least YOU'RE GOING TO THIS WEEK)

MONDAY : A GROUP OF HEDGEHOGS IS CALLED AN 'ARRAY' (WHO knew?!)

TUESDAY :

WEDNESDAY :

THURSDAY :

FRIDAY :

SATURDAY :

SUNDAY :

PEEP PEEP!

GOOGLE "USELESS FACTS" FOR SOME HELP.
NOW TRY and REMEMBER AT LEAST ONE
TO PASS ON AND TELL SOMEBODY ELSE.

FIND out ABOUT a POSITIVE STORY that HAS HAPPENED IN your LOCAL AREA

HEADLINE:

DATE:_____

STORY:_____

_____

_____

_____

_____

(MAKE YOUR OWN HAPPY NEWS IF YOU'RE STRUGGLING)

A FEW WAYS __WE__ COULD
MAKE THE WORLD
(OR SOMEBODY'S WORLD)
 A _little_ HAPPIER.

- __NOT BE A ~~DICK~~ HORRIBLE PERSON__

-

-

-

-

-

-

FIND out SOMETHING NEW about A FAMILY MEMBER

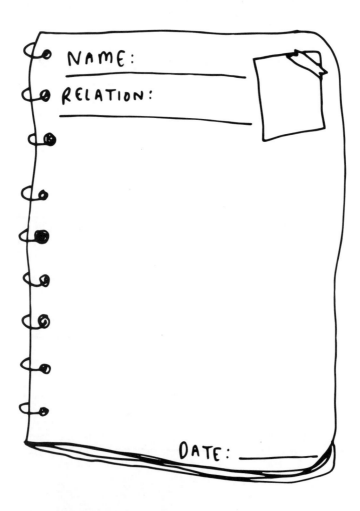

NAME:

RELATION:

DATE:

ONE FOR YOU

GREAT JOB!

you _____
_____

CONGRATULATIONS !! DATE: _____
(I'M SO PROUD I THINK I MIGHT PEE)
NAME: _____ YOU'RE AMAZING
AWARDED TO YOU BY: _____ ✂

GREAT JOB!

you _____
_____

CONGRATULATIONS !! DATE: _____
(I'M SO PROUD I THINK I MIGHT PEE)
NAME: _____ YOU'RE AMAZING
AWARDED TO YOU BY: _____ ✂

ONE FOR SOMEBODY YOU KNOW

A NEWS article /STORY THAT MADE ME CRY the <u>HAPPIEST</u> OF TEARS

SHARE IT OR TELL SOMEONE ABOUT IT

NO MATTER HOW HAPPY
you THINK A PERSON IS...
THERE's always a STORY
BEHIND each ONE of
THOSE ASSUMPTIONS.

you have NO IDEA
WHAT THAT PERSON
has BEEN THROUGH,
(OR IS GOING THROUGH),

SO BE KIND...
ALWAYS.

I AM SO SUPER PROUD of my _____ FOR:

☆ GETTING HIS/HER dream JOB

☆ OVERCOMING HIS/HER fear of

_____

☆ GETTING over IT

☆ BEING an ABSOLUTE dream BABE

☆ LEARNING HOW TO MAKE A GOOD CUP OF TEA / COFFEE

☆ MAKING a TINY HUMAN

☆ DOING that THING HE/SHE NEVER THOUGHT THEY COULD

☆

SPACE TO FOCUS ON <u>JUST</u> YOU

HOW'RE YOU FEELING?

REMEMBER TO TAKE A BREAK IF YOU NEED TO

WHAT'S BOTHERING YOU?

(OKAY, NOW SCRIBBLE IT OUT)

HAPPY SONG GUARANTEED TO MAKE ME smile...

by: _____

 PLAY IT LOUD
(OR QUIET... OR WHATEVER!)

SEND SOMEBODY A little
BOX OF HAPPY THINGS

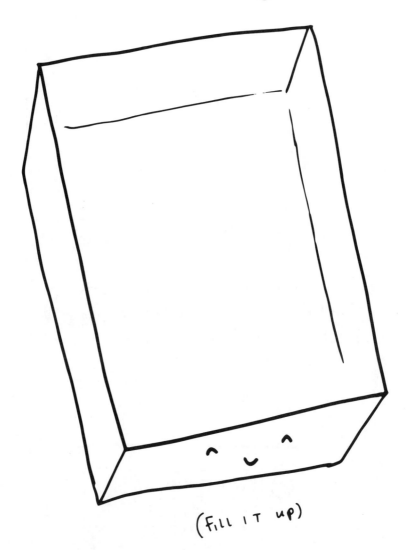

(FILL IT UP)

STUFF YOU
COULD INCLUDE:

- HOT CHOCOLATE & MARSHMALLOWS
- TINY HANDWRITTEN MESSAGE
- NOTEBOOK & PENS
- CANDY / SNACKS
- A FEW OF THEIR
  FAVORITE things
- SMILEY BALLOON
- lovely MEMORY

SEND a *lovely* MESSAGE

WHAT WAS the loveliest THING
that SOMEBODY HAS DONE FOR you
(THAT DIDN'T INVOLVE MATERIALISTIC STUFF)?

NEXT TIME YOU THINK OF SOMEONE
(OR YOU'RE REMINDED OF THEM) WRITE
THEM A POSTCARD...

HELLO _____

I JUST WANTED TO LET YOU KNOW I
THOUGHT OF YOU ON _____

_____ REMINDED ME
OF YOU AND IT MADE ME HAPPY
BECAUSE _____

_____

LOVE FROM _____

_____

WRITE DOWN A <u>MASSIVE</u>
GLOBAL PROBLEM that
HASN'T BEEN SOLVED YET...

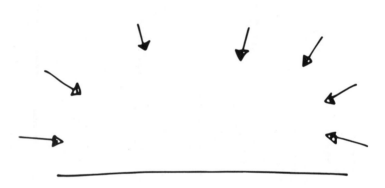

...NOW SCRIBBLE IT OUT

WRITE down a TINY
little THING that you CAN
DO TO MAKE YOUR IMMEDIATE
SURROUNDINGS A BIT MORE
ᗏPOSITIVEᗎ

_____

~~EAT CAKE~~
e.g., ~~MAKE BED~~
BUY SOMEONE A SNACK
TELL SOMEONE THEY'RE
lovely

I GENUINELY believe THAT HAPPINESS IS CONTAGIOUS and A SINGLE SMILE COULD CHANGE a PERSON'S WHOLE DAY.

IF your mood was a Room
Full of PEOPLE... HOW HAPPY
WOULD IT BE?

COMPLETE the FACES...

HOW ARE you FEELING?

TRY **LISTENING** a little **MORE** AND TALKING a LITTLE **LESS** TODAY

WHAT DID you learn?

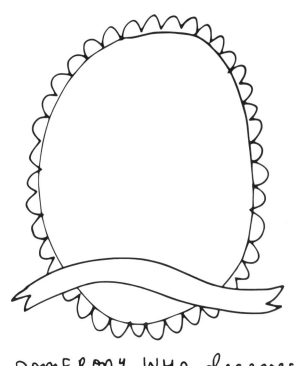

SOMEBODY WHO deserves
to be <u>HEADLINE NEWS</u>:

_____

_____

_____

_____

_____

_____

(ANIMALS ALSO WELCOME)

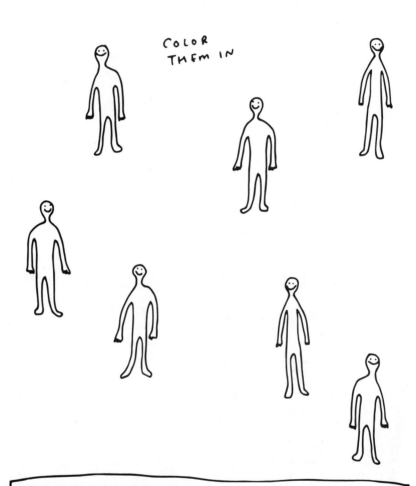

THE SMILE AT a STRANGER GAME

COLOR THEM IN

HOW MANY PEOPLE CAN you SURPRISE BY SIMPLY SMILING at THEM?

(ALSO INCLUDES WAVING and SAYING HELLO)

THINGS you COULD SAY TO SOMEBODY WHO'S NOT FEELING SO GREAT...

THIS IS CRAP

~~CHEER UP~~

JUST KNOW I'M HERE

~~YOU'LL BE FINE~~

YOU'RE INCREDIBLY BRAVE

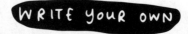

WRITE YOUR OWN

FAVORITE NEWS ARTICLE EVER

IF YOU HAVE THE POWER to make someone HAPPY, DO IT! THE WORLD NEEDS MORE OF THAT

If you could pack a tiny CARE PACKAGE for a HOMELESS PERSON WHAT WOULD YOU INCLUDE?

IDEAS...

CANNED FOOD / DRY CEREAL / DRIED FRUIT / NUTS /
HOT CHOCOLATE / SANITARY PRODUCTS / HAND WARMERS /
GLOVES / HAT / TISSUES / WIPES, ETC.

YOU MATTER

FILL THE BOX

(NOW, TRY DONATING IN REAL LIFE!)

STUFF that PEOPLE ~~could~~
SHOULD do TO MAKE ME

SMILE

- SEND ACTUAL real MAIL ✉ ‹
- BAKE ME A CAKE (or buy
  me A CAKE, I'M NOT Fussy)
-
  _____

-
  _____

-
  _____

-
  _____

-
  _____

COULD YOU DO ANY OF THESE TO
MAKE SOMEONE ELSE HAPPY?

PEOPLE YOU COULD TRY TO SPEAK / WRITE to MORE:

NAME:

ADDRESS:

NO.

NAME:

ADDRESS:

NO.

NAME:

ADDRESS:

NO.

NAME:

ADDRESS:

NO.

WRITE DOWN an INSPIRING
STORY you HEARD ABOUT
this WEEK...

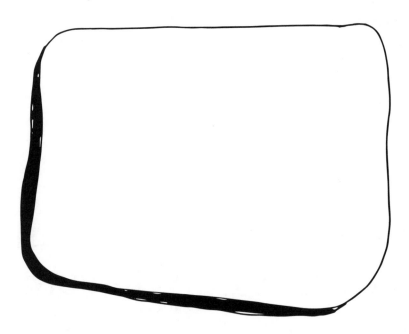

COULD you DO SOMETHING
~~EQUALLY~~ NEARLY AS
WONDERFUL?

PEOPLE I'M GRATEFUL TO HAVE IN MY LIFE...

FILL THE PAGE WITH WONKY HEART MESSAGES

you ARE LOVED

WRITE A LOVELY message
on this CHECK FOR A WAITER/
WAITRESS (or on an actual CHECK!)

(CUT THESE OUT and LEAVE THEM IN PUBLIC)

✂ - - - - - - -

KEEP
SMILING

☀

YOU'RE
INCREDIBLE
and
BRAVE

TAKE SOME
time to
focus ON
YOU

YOU'RE
like
ACTUAL
MAGIC

THE WORLD
IS FULL of
MAGIC
☆ and ☆
WONDER

(WRITE YOUR OWN)

TAKE A PHOTO OF YOUR
HAPPY PLACE (STICK IT BELOW)

(A REAL PHOTO!)

my BEST
(and WORST)
JOKE

SOMEBODY ELSE'S

BEST/WORST
JOKE

(taxi drivers, FRIEND, or WHOEVER)

TAKE a FRIEND or FAMILY MEMBER out FOR LUNCH... or a drink... OR FOR CAKE...OR FOR no reason whatsoever!

(WHO NEEDS an EXCUSE TO EAT CAKE?)

FIND OUT a STORY they've NEVER TOLD YOU BEFORE
(WRITE IT ABOVE)

A MESSAGE that MADE me THE HAPPIEST

DATE:

Go (ever so slightly) out of your WAY TO HELP SOMEBODY THIS WEEK (CHECK THEM OFF)...

HELP WITH STROLLER/ LUGGAGE UP/DOWN STAIRS

OFFER TO HELP ELDERLY PERSON WITH HEAVY BAGS

GIVE UP YOUR SEAT

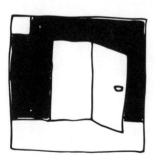

HOLD DOOR OPEN FOR SOMEONE

LET SOMEBODY GO IN FRONT OF YOU IN LINE

CHAT WITH A HOMELESS PERSON (OR ANY NEW PERSON)

REASONS

I'M SO GLAD

you EXIST:

NAME:

- _____
  _____

- _____
  _____

- _____
  _____

- _____
  _____

- _____
  _____

(TELL THEM!!)

♡ **REMEMBER** THE COMPLIMENTS
♡ you RECEIVE...

FROM A FRIEND:

FROM A RANDOM PERSON:

FROM A FAMILY MEMBER:

COMPLIMENT SOMEBODY! REMEMBER HOW THE COMPLIMENTS MADE YOU FEEL, THEN PASS SOME ON...

EVERYTHING
IS OKAY

YOU'RE DOING
GREAT

THE HAPPY NEWS

JUST CHECKING IN...

ARE YOU HAPPY ??

[ ] YES [ ] NO

SOMETHING REALLY TINY YOU COULD DO TO MAKE YOURSELF SMILE...

Go and DO IT!!

CREATE a WALL OF LOVING
MESSAGES you'd like TO SEE
WHILE WALKING DOWN THE STREET

NOTICE STUFF THAT makes you SMILE ALL DAY LONG (WRITE THEM DOWN) AND USE ONE or MORE TO MAKE SOME ONE else HAPPY

FILL THE WHOLE PAGE

IF YOU COULD WRITE A KIND
MESSAGE TO ANY FIVE PEOPLE,
WHAT WOULD YOU WANT TO SAY?

1.

2.

3.

4.

5.

FIND A **HAPPY NEWS**
ARTICLE FROM the DAY (OR WEEK)
you WERE BORN:

BEST DAY EVER

COLOR ME IN

WRITE A *letter* TO your train
conductor /pilot / taxi or bus driver

DEAR _____

Thank you FOR GETTING ME
HOME SAFELY...

(leave it for them to find)

A STREET PERFORMER
WHO MADE you smile:

SONG:
(OR LYRICS)
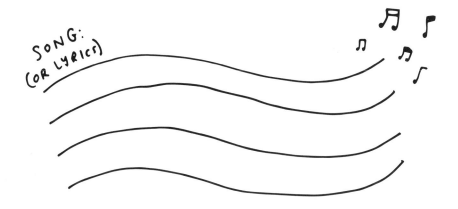

INSTRUMENT:

SPEND SOME TIME
looking UP at THE
SKY RATHER than
down at your SCREEN

WHAT DO YOU SEE?

THANK
Somebody
TODAY

NAME:

_____

☐ For being them

☐ SOMETHING THEY DID

_____

☐ WHAT they DO

_____

☐ SOMETHING they SAID

_____

_____

THESE ARE a FEW of my FAVORITE THINGS:

^ MOST

FIND OUT YOUR BEST FRIEND'S FAVORITE THINGS (FILL THE PAGE)

THIS PAGE WILL COME IN SUPER HANDY ON THEIR BIRTHDAY (OR THE NEXT TIME THEY'RE FEELING CRAPPY)

WHAT WAS that THING you
SHARED online BECAUSE IT
MADE you SMILE?

WHAT'S ON YOUR MIND?

(TELL them I TOLD You
TO, IF ANYONE ASKS)

WRITE a letter (OR EMAIL) TO A SCHOOLTEACHER WHO helped/ INSPIRED YOU

Dear

FIND an EMAIL address FOR the SCHOOL...they'll MOST LIKELY BE ABLE TO PASS IT ON FOR YOU

DRAW a BIG felt-tip RAINBOW
with a tiny MESSAGE of HOPE
UNDERNEATH IT...

#MAKESOMEONEHAPPY

(STICK IT TO A LAMPPOST)   MESSAGE

WRITE a *letter* TO YOUR
EX-BEST FRIEND
(or somebody else you ONCE KNEW)

hi _____

I know it's BEEN a while BUT
I JUST WANTED TO SEND a little
MESSAGE TO SAY _____

_____

_____

_____

THERE ARE NO HARD FEELINGS

_____

_____

                    _____

DESCRIBE A STRANGER YOU MET ONE time:

(nick)
NAME: _____

THE MOST
FASCINATING
THING ABOUT
THEM:

↑ PICTURE
FROM
MEMORY

DRAW AS MANY RAINBOWS AS
POSSIBLE... AND THEN DRAW
LOADS MORE

WRITE A "THANKS FOR BEING YOU"
MESSAGE TO A STRANGER WHO MAY
      NEED TO HEAR IT TODAY...

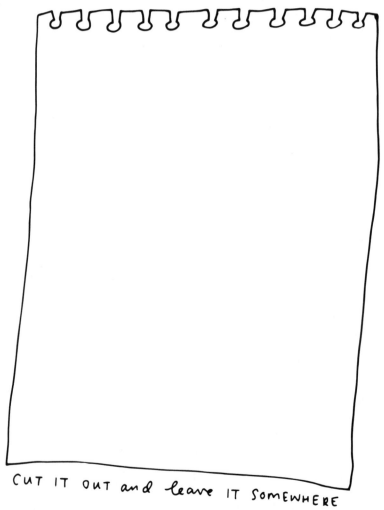

CUT IT OUT and leave IT SOMEWHERE

IF YOU COULD SEND SOME STUFF
OFF in MAGIC BUBBLES TO BE
FIXED /MADE BETTER
(OR TO MAKE DISAPPEAR)...
WHAT WOULD THEY BE?

PEEP
PEEP

FIND THE MOST WONDERFUL
animal STORY IN THE NEWS
THIS WEEK:

HEADLINE: eeeep!

draw / DESCRIBE / PASTE here

What CRISIS HAVE you SURVIVED or WHAT CHALLENGES HAVE you OVERCOME?

YOUR WISDOM GAINED COULD HELP SOMEBODY ELSE.
VOLUNTEER WITH A CHARITY OR COMMUNITY ORGANIZATION
OR JUST REACH OUT TO SOMEBODY YOU KNOW WHO IS
GOING THROUGH A SIMILAR SITUATION.

NEXT time...

(FILL OUT the RESULTS)

YOU'RE IN A RESTAURANT

SEND YOUR COMPLIMENTS TO THE CHEF

YOU'RE IN A HOTEL

with Compliments

FILL OUT THE FEEDBACK FORM

YOU SEE YOUR DELIVERYMAN

GIVE HIM A SNACK/DRINK

IT'S RAINING

BUY A STRANGER AN UMBRELLA

YOU SEE A DOG/CAT

PET IT

YOU'RE AT THE MOVIES

BUY SOMEONE POPCORN

YOU DO SPRING CLEANING

DONATE TO CHARITY

YOU GET FAST FOOD

BUY SOMETHING EXTRA FOR A HOMELESS PERSON

YOU SEE SOME CHEAP FLOWERS

BUY THEM & GIVE TO A STRANGER OR leave FOR SOMEONE TO FIND

YOU SEE YOUR FRIEND

IT'S WARM

GET SOMEONE AN ICE CREAM

BRING THEM A lovely PHOTO OF THE TWO OF YOU - GET A COPY FOR YOU TOO! (STICK IT ABOVE)

MAKE A PLAYLIST OF SONGS
that MAKE you THE HAPPIEST

TRACKS:

HAPPY PLAYLIST PEEP PEEP PEEP

(SHARE IT WITH SOMEONE... OR
MAKE IT INTO A CD... DO PEOPLE
STILL DO THAT?!)

FOR EVERY BIT OF truly
HORRIBLE NEWS there's AN
ABSOLUTELY MAGICAL.
STORY TO COUNTERACT IT...

STICK a HAPPY NEWS STORY
OVER A NEGATIVE Story ABOVE
(TRY HUFFPOST + GOODNEWS NETWORK)

FIND A PERSON,
CAMPAIGN, OR CHARITY THAT
IS MAKING this WORLD
A BETTER PLACE

MAKE them
INTO A STAR

WE like
THESE
PEOPLE

GIVE SOMEBODY YOUR FULL ATTENTION

WHAT DID you learn? ANYTHING...

TRY NOT TO BE DISTRACTED BY YOUR PHONE OR WHATEVER else AND REALLY LISTEN, I PROMISE IT HELPS

BUZZ BUZZ

BE A TOURIST IN YOUR OWN
TOWN / CITY - VISIT SOMEWHERE
OR SOMETHING NEW

WHAT CAN you SEE?

TAKE A TINY BIT
OF TIME TO APPRECIATE
that you've lived
NEARBY AND NEVER
SEEN OR NOTICED
THIS PLACE.

If YOU COULD WRITE a
NEWS HEADLINE that MAGICALLY
MADE that thing HAPPEN,
WHAT WOULD IT BE?

COLOR ME IN

FILL THE BOXES WITH TINY PICK-ME-UPS

CUT THEM OUT, FOLD THEM UP, AND POP THEM INTO A JAR TO
SAVE FOR A BAD DAY OR TO GIVE TO A FRIEND WHEN THEY NEED IT.

COLOR ME IN

WE OFTEN WORRY
SO MUCH THAT WE
WON'T KNOW The "right"
THING TO SAY TO A
FRIEND OR LOVED one
having a DIFFICULT TIME...
WHEN ACTUALLY THEY
usually JUST NEED to
know you're there.
MAYBE THINK OF WHAT you
would want some one to say
To you IN A SIMILAR SITUATION.

WRITE YOURSELF a LITTLE MESSAGE YOU'D WANT TO HEAR on YOUR DARKEST day

THINGS WILL BE OKAY

(YOU'RE GOING TO GET THROUGH IT, etc.)

BEING KIND NEVER NEEDS
TO TAKE UP TOO MUCH
TIME OR EFFORT (and
   CERTAINLY NOT MONEY)

- [ ] SMILE at SOMEONE

- [ ] PAY SOMEONE a COMPLIMENT

- [ ] SEND SOMEONE a CARD

- [ ] VOLUNTeeR AT A LOCAL
  SHELTER/SOUP KITCHEN

- [ ] TAG SOMEONE IN A FUNNY
  VIDEO OR A PICTURE OF
  a FLUFFY PANDA

THINK OF SOME OF YOUR OWN...

☐
_____

☐
_____

☐
_____

☐
_____

☐
_____

I hereby solemnly swear that...

I will NOT compare myself

TO A STRANGER ON INSTAGRAM

TAKE A PHOTO OF THIS PAGE and SHARE IT ONLINE
TO REMIND OTHERS THAT SOCIAL MEDIA ISN'T REAL life

THANK SOMEBODY WHO UNKNOWINGLY
HELPED YOU ON A <u>NOT SO GREAT DAY</u>
(AUTHOR / MUSICIAN / SOMEONE FAMOUS)

SOMEBODY WHO'S MADE A DIFFERENCE...

TINY IDEA:
SEND THEM A *lovely* TWEET - THEY OFTEN
GET A WHOLE LOAD OF CRAP SENT TO THEM
AND MOST OF THEM ARE JUST *like* ME + YOU

BE GRATEFUL

WRITE a list OF STUFF
YOU'RE GRATEFUL FOR TODAY

_____

_____

_____

_____

_____

_____

_____

ASK SOMEBODY else WHAT
THEY'RE GRATEFUL FOR

_____

_____

_____

_____

_____

_____

_____

DO YOU HAVE
ANY IN COMMON?

It comes DOWN To us As
INDIVIDUALS and HOW WE
treat EACH OTHER... WE
MUST NOT let THOSE who
RUN OUR TOWNS or COUNTRIES
TAKE AWAY the MUTUAL
RESPECT we should ALL
HAVE FOR ONE another.

If you WERE ELECTED PRIME MINISTER / PRESIDENT / KING / QUEEN WHAT WOULD be the FIRST THING YOU DID?

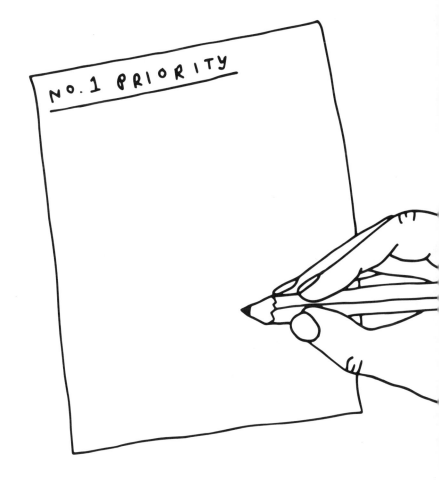

NO.1 PRIORITY

hi, I just wanted
To say... I THINK
you'RE DOING a
GREAT JOB!

SERIOUSLY,
you'RE like
ACTUAL
MAGIC.

POST a PHOTO OF THIS PAGE and TAG a FEW OF YOUR FAVORITE PEOPLE #MAKESOMEONEHAPPY

A LITTLE NOTE TO THE PERSON WHO'S ALWAYS MAKING everybody ELSE **HAPPY** (THEY GET SAD TOO SOMETIMES)

·SPRINKLE·
SOME SECRETIVE KINDNESS...

IT'S BOUND TO RESTORE SOMEONE'S
FAITH IN HUMANITY A TINY BIT.

☐ leave A LOVELY NOTE ON A CAR

☐ leave SOME CHANGE IN A VENDING
MACHINE OR PARKING METER

☐ leave YOUR NEWSPAPER/MAGAZINE
OR BOOK ON PUBLIC TRANSPORT

☐ leave a COFFEE FOR YOUR COLLEAGUE

OTHER STUFF YOU COULD DO:

☐

☐

☐

TRY
NOT TO
GET CAUGHT

BUCKET
loads Of
LOVE

REMEMBER THAT FRIEND WHO WENT through A
REALLY DIFFICULT TIME A little WHILE AGO?
SEND THEM SOME LOVE and REMIND THEM you
HAVEN'T FORGOTTEN - THEY'LL PROBABLY STILL
HAVE SOME RUBBISH DAYS.

DO SOMETHING with a FRIEND
that NEITHER of you HAVE
DONE BEFORE

WHAT DID you SEE/
HEAR / Do...?

DATE:

WE MUST CONTINUE to
FOCUS on the POSITIVES,
the EVERYDAY HEROES,
TINY MIRACLES and
MOMENTS OF PURE JOY.

BE KIND TO YOUR ENEMIES.
WRITE DOWN **ONE THING**
that's GOOD ABOUT THE PERSON
you like THE LEAST

...SEE, THAT WASN'T SO BAD!

TAKE SOME TIME TO NOTICE THE SIMILARITIES

COLOR THEM IN

WE have FAR MORE in COMMON WITH EACH other THAN things THAT divide us

WHAT'S YOUR FAVORITE BOOK?

TITLE:

AUTHOR:

WHAT MAKES IT YOUR FAVORITE?

WHO COULD BENEFIT FROM READING IT?
(COULD YOU LEND IT TO THEM?)

FIND OUT SOME REALLY IMPORTANT INFO

about a FAMILY MEMBER:

WHO:

THEIR
ADDRESS:

FAVORITE
CHOCOLATE:

FAVORITE
CANDY:

WORST DAY
OF the YEAR:

BEST DAY
OF THE YEAR:

THEIR PHONE
NUMBER:

FAVORITE
COLOR:

FIND OUT SOME REALLY IMPORTANT INFO

about a FRIEND

WHO :
_____

THEIR
ADDRESS:

FAVORITE
CHOCOLATE:

FAVORITE
CANDY:

WORST DAY
OF the YEAR:

BEST DAY
OF THE YEAR:

THEIR PHONE
NUMBER:

FAVORITE
COLOR:

NOW you CAN SEND THEM AN EXTRA-SPECIAL & lovely SURPRISE ♥

YAY!

DRAW A SCRIBBLE that
represents How your mind
CURRENTLY FEELS

□ PRETTY GOOD   □ PRETTY STRESSED

SOMETHING I SAW TODAY that made my HEART GO All KINDS of fuzzy:

HOW MANY
POSITIVE SIGNS
did you see today?

SMILE
YOU'RE
ON 😊
CAMERA

LEARN and REMEMBER SOMEONE'S NAME — ONE you DON'T REALLY NEED TO, but it WOULD be NICE TO.

(e.g., YOUR LOCAL STORE OWNER, MAIL CARRIER, OFFICE CLEANER, etc.)

REPEAT their NAME on the PAGE until you've FILLED it (OR UNTIL IT STARTS TO FEEL a little WEIRD)

MAKE THE WORLD A BETTER PLACE

(ADD all YOUR FAVORITE THINGS)

VISIT A BRAND NEW PLACE

STICK HERE...
A RECEIPT, POST-CARD, WRAPPER, TICKET, PASS, PAPER BAG, COUPON, FLUFF, MENU, TOKEN, leaf, FLOWER, BILL, BUSINESS CARD, PHOTO, CHEWING GUM, MONEY, PIECE OF GRASS, FLYER, POSTER, ENVELOPE, STAMP, OR ANY OTHER RANDOM CRAP YOU CAN FIND

WHERE did you GO?

_____

☐ WILL GO BACK

☐ WILL ABSOLUTELY PROBABLY NEVER GO AGAIN

(EVEN IF IT DOESN'T
FEEL like IT SOMETIMES)

MY OWN HAPPY SELF-CARE KIT INCLUDES:

SOMETHING COMFORTING

WORDS OF WISDOM I'D SAY TO SOMEONE ELSE IN THIS SITUATION

ACTIVITY

PERSON I CAN CALL ON (LITERALLY)

GUILTY PLEASURE

HAPPY PLACE

FAVORITE FOOD

mmm!

WHAT WAS the BEST
thing you learned WHILE
DOING THIS BOOK?

_____

_____

_____

FAVORITE moment
that CAME from MAKING
SOMEONE HAPPY?

_____

_____

_____

LIST *five*

THINGS YOU'RE GOING
TO TRY TO DO MORE OF:

1. _____

2. _____

3. _____

4. _____

5. _____

THANK YOU TO MY MUM AND DAD WHO HAVE
BROUGHT SO MUCH HAPPINESS TO MY WORLD, FOR
MAKING ME BELIEVE in MY DREAMS and GIVING
ME the WORK ETHIC TO MAKE THOSE DREAMS a
REALITY. I WILL BE FOREVER GRATEFUL TO YOU BOTH
... AND to MY BIG BROTHER, TOM, FOR ALWAYS
MAKING ME LAUGH, I LOVE YOU ALL. ♥

TO NIALL FOR NEVER FAILING to SUPPORT
ABSOLUTELY everything I do, AND FOR
MAKING ME SMILE... ALWAYS.

THANK YOU TO AMANDA SHIH (MY EDITOR) and
EVERYBODY ELSE WHO HAS BELIEVED in me and
MY SILLY LITTLE IDEAS/SCRIBBLES ON this SLIGHTLY
SURREAL BUT GLITTER-FILLED JOURNEY - YOU'RE THE BEST.

TO MY FRIENDS and FAMILY WHO FILL MY WORLD
with LAUGHTER, love, PIZZA, and STUFF - I LOVE you.

LAST BUT NOT least... THANK YOU TO ANYONE WHO
HAS BOUGHT SOMETHING OF MINE, liked/SHARED/
SUPPORTED ABSOLUTELY ANYTHING I HAVE done -
YOU'RE THE REASON I'M ABLE TO DO all OF this
AND MAKE MORE PEOPLE SMILE along the WAY.

ALSO a SHOUT-OUT TO NEIL BUCHANAN and
ANYBODY else WHO HAS INSPIRED me IN
TINY and huge WAYS.

love from emily x

ABOUT the AUTHOR

EMILY COXHEAD is a fluffy-haired BRITISH DESIGNER, illustrator, and HAPPY THING maker. FOUNDER OF THE HAPPY NEWSPAPER, emily AIMS TO BRING a bit OF SUNSHINE to the WORLD. SHE has NO IDEA what she's DOING... but SHE'S HAVING a lovely TIME.

@EMILYCOXHEAD
WWW.EMILYCOXHEAD.com
WWW.THEHAPPYNEWSPAPER.com
#MAKESOMEONEHAPPY